The Phoenix Living Poets

———————

THE MOUNTAIN LION

Poets Published in
The Phoenix Living Poets Series

★

JAMES AITCHISON

ALEXANDER BAIRD · ALAN BOLD

R. H. BOWDEN · FREDERICK BROADIE

GEORGE MACKAY BROWN

HAYDEN CARRUTH · JOHN COTTON

JENNIFER COUROUCLI

GLORIA EVANS DAVIES

PATRIC DICKINSON

TOM EARLEY · D. J. ENRIGHT

JOHN FULLER · DAVID GILL

PETER GRUFFYDD

J. C. HALL · MOLLY HOLDEN

JOHN HORDER · P. J. KAVANAGH

RICHARD KELL · LAURIE LEE

LAURENCE LERNER

CHRISTOPHER LEVENSON

EDWARD LOWBURY · NORMAN MacCAIG

ROY McFADDEN

JAMES MERRILL · RUTH MILLER

LESLIE NORRIS · ROBERT PACK

ARNOLD RATTENBURY

ADRIENNE RICH · JON SILKIN

JON STALLWORTHY

GILLIAN STONEHAM

EDWARD STOREY · TERENCE TILLER

SYDNEY TREMAYNE

LOTTE ZURNDORFER

THE
MOUNTAIN LION

by

JON MANCHIP WHITE

CHATTO AND WINDUS

THE HOGARTH PRESS

1971

Published by
Chatto & Windus Ltd
with The Hogarth Press Ltd
42 William IV Street
London W.C.2
*
Clarke, Irwin & Co. Ltd

Distributed in the United States of America
by Wesleyan University Press

ISBN: 0 8195 7037 0

Printed in Great Britain by
Lewis Reprints Limited
London and Tonbridge

For
ROBERT CONQUEST

Yn Aber Cuawc yt ganant gogeu
ar gangheu blodeuawc
gwae glaf ae clyw yn vodawc

Contents

THE MOUNTAIN LION

For eight sweet years I ambled in the pines
 And struck the silly sheep and crunched their bones

The huddled herds were frightened of their shadows
 Living was red and fat among the meadows

I slid between the soft flanks of the cattle
 And hooked them with a claw as hard as metal

Wet were my jaws and damp my pizzle
 Slick my pelt and streaked my muzzle

Nothing so good can last for ever
 They tracked me lapping at the river

Three of the dogs I ripped to bits
 Six bullets whacked me in the guts

They peeled my tousled hide and scooped it out
 And gave the scavengers the marbled meat

The skin they took and draped around a post
 And nailed it through the skull to hold it fast

My limbs spreadeagled sideways in derision
 Spiked on the barbs to keep them in position

Even in death I stay a shape of wrath
 A grinning terror strung beside the path

And though I shrivel in the noonday glare
 While hot winds nibble at my mangy fur

My brown ghost holds my ancient realm as fast
 As if my fangs had never turned to dust

My footprint stamped as roundly on the rocks
   As when I stalked the sheep and broke their necks

And though the pinetrees and the mountains fall
   A pungent essence will remain to dwell
A pride and presence stalking on the hill

THE SILVER SWIMMER

Who was the silver swimmer who flipped towards me
   Touching the tips of his fingers to mine
As I reached surface of the sunlit Rio Grande

   Who was the ebony horseman who kept stride for stride
                                   behind me
Slithering between the mesquite and the cholla
   As I rode across the silence of the noonday desert

Who was the grey ghost hiding in the mist
   Waving his giant limbs in time to mine
As I stood on the summit of the Sierra Blanca

   Who was the fellow in the glass above the basin
In every motel between Phoenix and Galveston
   Grinning and sticking his tongue out and baring his teeth
Dapping soap on his cheeks and sliding out of sight

That man has followed me as long as I remember
   Never saying a word except sometimes in the mountains
When I shout and a muffled voice shouts back to me

   Although I seldom bother to trouble my head about him
Recently I have been wondering about this other self or double
   Closer than a brother

He seems contented enough and playful and volatile
   Nicely active and pleasantly discreet
Appearing so well-disposed I never worry about him

I will let him live in his azure film of water
   And the soft-shelled skin of the yellow desert
I will let him skate on the mercurial surface of my mirror

One day we are bound to greet and confront each other
   Merging in a moment
Parting company in a flash

   Until that second I shall try to keep my distance
Forget he is mysterious and disturbing
   Ask no questions about him

   I have no urge to meet him in the flesh

THE RANCHES OF TAOS

It took me many years to come to terms with him
  His ideas were often shrill and his pages silly
                or slipshod
Even today there was laughter mingled with the pity
                and respect
  Typical of Lawrence to have a shrine instead of a
                simple grave

Today I paid my apology and made amends
  Drove the dirt road between the protective peaks
Climbed the path to the beckoning plaster phoenix
  A decorous little Etruscan tomb in a pinewood
                clearing

His women have buried Don Lorenzo well in Taos
  A seemly lodgment for his blown and battered ashes
A low plain altar and a small stained window
  One of his own innocuous water colours

Outside the pillared entrance the inseparable touch
                of comedy
  Frieda sprawled at the threshold beneath a handsome
                slab
The florid Richtofen arms akimbo at its head
  The mild resigned third spouse wedged between wall
                and headstone

Frau Professor Weekly guarding her brood and vetting
                the visitors
  A tawny protective eye on her menfolk even in death
Bracelet of bright hair about the bone
  The big broad mastiff bitch faithful at her master's
                feet

O yes Don Lorenzo that resplendent woman has buried you
well
   In the high pure lacy air like Tuscany
Over and over a random insistent phrase rustled my mind
   Rest rest it whispered *rest perturbed spirit*

Here at the bitter end harsh Nature and man relented
   Here at last you enjoy a little late luck
After wandering in Sardinia Sicily Ceylon Australia Mexico
   You have found a noble and welcoming patch of earth

After the bad start in the sullen rainy country
   Passion in clay and flame among the clods
You have reached a lofty region of valley and mountain
   Serpentine canyons of the Rio Grande

You lie in the embrasure of the pueblos
   Yesterday at the Corn Dance at Santo Domingo
I lifted a prayer to the sunburned gods for you among
the kivas
   Brown feet pounding the ground as a whole town danced
around the hot adobe houses

The sickly son of the Eastwood miner delving deep in the
darkness
   Driving a powerful shaft into hidden places
Bringing a glistening black trove to light with broken nails
and blood on every lump
   Pioneer undeterred by the fearful risks of the rockfall

Let me give you thanks and make amends
   Brave collier worn out early attacking the obdurate
rockface
You deserve your clean white shrine high in the winelike
air
   No explorer ever merited a finer monument

14

The buried slot of the river caresses the sparkling sky
  The pinewood scents are holy and free from sweat and
                    grit
The slopes are sown with sunflowers as thick as stooks
                    of corn
  Rest rest perturbed spirit rest rest rest

And yet as I stand on this fragrant brilliant slope
  I turn my head towards the turbulent east
Remembering our far and clouded land
  Our nurse and nanny whose fretful clasp we fled from

You could stand it there now less than you stood it then
  A dazed disheartened people nagged by bumptious and
                    threadbare ideologues
The bottom dog clambering mangily to the top
  Let us defend ourselves from the bottom dog with its
                    mean growl and yellow teeth

In my humbler way I came from a countryside blackened
                    and gutted
  Burrowed in the maze of ancient dusty galleries
Sought release at last in higher wider ground
  Prospects of space and perspectives of liberation

A long way from this wild and radiant hill
  The mournful tender skies of Nottingham
A long way from the murmur in the pines
  The shires of England with their strong sad music

Magnanimous shade as you rove your fortunate mountain
  I ask forgiveness from you for our ungrateful country
Before we must ask in turn to be forgiven
  By a land too dear to us to need her children's
                    forgiveness

And so I linger an hour before I travel on
  Seeking to give and receive a benediction
I will pluck a sunflower and carry it into the shrine
  I pick a sunflower and lay it on your altar

THE LADY AND THE DOVES

Farewell farewell my forty doves
    My drops of milk among the leaves
    My curds and whey upon the grass
    My strokes of snow across the pool
    My crumbs of icing on the paths
    My unstrung pearls among the roses
    My lily petals on the eaves
Farewell farewell my forty dives

Farewell farewell my forty doves
    The dry seed rustles in my palm
    The paper whisper of a wing
    The gripping of a nervous claw
    The warm note fondled in the throat
    The dipping of a gentle neck
    The rattle of a harmless beak
Farewell farewell my forty doves

Farewell farewell my forty doves
    You fastened on my hand to feed
    You loved the summer days and flourished
    You feared the frosty nights and perished
    You wandered to my door to die
    You lay on straw inside my kitchen
    You closed your round mild eye and sighed
Farewell farewell my forty doves

Farewell farewell my forty doves
    What do you know of griefs and absence
    What do you know of worlds away
    What do you know of separation
    What do you know of long goodbyes
    What do you know of ships and oceans
    What do you know of foreign ranges
Farewell farewell my forty doves

17

Farewell farewell my forty doves
    My lily petals on the eaves
    My unstrung pearls among the roses
    My crumbs of icing on the paths
    My strokes of snow across the pool
    My curds and whey upon the grass
    My drops of milk among the leaves
Farewell farewell my forty doves

BRANDBERG

It crests from the plain on the track between
                    Walvis Bay and Otjiwarongo
    a blackbrown peak settled on the flat stone
                    desert
        seen through the gritty windshield a hundred
                    miles away
            as the truck goes thrumming along the wide
                    scraped road

Over an hour it seems to hover motionless
    a single and solitary cloud stationed above its
                    summit
        its broadbaked slopes littered with redscarred
                    boulders
            blocks of rock scored with untransliterable
                    runes

At the heart of the enigmatic triangle of granite
    a cave with a painted frieze of roving Bushmen
        led by a slender figure with ashen limbs
            a strange White Lady or Diana of the veld

The Brandberg or the Fire Mountain
    shrine of the delicate fleet-limbed honey-skinned
                    nomads
        holy hill of a thousand generations
            revered and worshipped by our first shy ancestors

Fire Mountain ignorant of prayers and praises
    of hopes and fears or waking or weeping
        of knowing and caring or breathing or brooding
            of being a mountain or being a mountain in Africa

Brandberg ignorant of being the Brandberg
    of being an agglomeration of rock
        of being a monument or a landmark
            of having a sanctuary hidden in its heart

Then why do I linger on the verge of sleep
    watching the Brandberg hover on the desert
        a presence planted at the gates of oblivion
            on the dusty journey to the valley of sleep

Pyramids of Khufu and Mycerinus on the scored and
                    crystalline plateau
    Floridas towards Deming and Lordsburg under silk and
                    tortoiseshell sunsets
        white cone of Sierra Blanca presiding above
                    Ruidoso and Cloudcroft
            floating peak of the Fire Mountain across the
                    skimmering Namib

Nothing to a drowsy mind the indifference of the
                    mountain
    its heartlessness and stoniness
        hardness and remoteness
            nothing its lofty and olympian impassivity

Great shape folded in the geometry of the brain
    shape of grandeur in a giant landscape
        pillar at the threshold of the magic country
            majestic pylon at the boundary of the
                    kingdom of dreams

The girl in the lilac silk and silver kerchief
   Beside an open window with geraniums on the sill
Sunlight stroking the seed pearls in her hair
   Looks at a letter written in violet ink
A letter with ragged edges
   Smiling at what she reads

The letter dangles from her dimpled fingers
   A fat round diamond on the plump right thumb
Triangulates the light
   The small round belly beneath the swelling silk
In which the pink tips of the left hand linger
   Shows she is near her time

Beneath the window of the milky girl
   Four men with insolent moustaches and flowing hair
Their brave breasts glowing with brooches and brilliant sashes
   Laugh and swill foaming ale from pewter tankards
At a mahogany table with stained top and bulbous legs
   Their high-crowned high-plumed hats on the bench beside
                                                  them

The courtyard is paved with diamond-shapes tiles
   Red and buff in herring-bone patterns
Vines on trellises throw shadows like velvet spearheads
   At pears and nectarines espaliered against the warm
                                             purple brick
   Like oozy crucifixions
Bay trees in neat square tubs
   Clipped and fretted into glossy globes

A peaches-and-cream maid spills ale from a frothy crock
   Wriggling and giggling as the topers pinch her bottom
Away in the corner behind the door with the carven angels
   Two men in maroon cloaks whisper behind their hands

21

And raise their slender glasses in a toast to love or
                              treachery
   While an old yellow dog slumbers in a patch of sun
A butterfly opens its wide indigo wings on the cage of the
                              bird from the Indies

Severed by glass
   I stand in my sober suit in front of the sweet scene
The morning sour and damp and the cold rain falling
   On the saturated streets outside with the fuming traffic
I strain my eyes and ears
   But the happy voices do not seem to carry
To my far-off city

Where now is the wine-drenched swashing corner of the universe
   Fat and sleek and pert as a scissored bay-tree
Where drinkers roar their boozy fruity randy laughter
   A girl at the window smiles at her violet letter
A maid squeals at the bold hand caressing the globe of her rump
   Conspirators sip and discuss their slow and stately treason

What does the painted butterfly dream on the sun-warmed metal
                              of the cage
   What images lost and scattered are pattering through the old
                              dog's brain
What faint and foreign tongue is the bantering talk in
   What mote and dot of dust still holds the cheerful vanished
                              lechers
The varnished scene caught in the amber and dripping honey of
                              the sunlight
   The sunlight with the honey and the globe of the mellow
                              amber

INTRODUCTION AND ALLEGRO

Cynghanedd between Fort Stockton
and Corpus Christi

He lies in the lee of the small grey church
    on the scarp
In a little bedraggled graveyard beneath a
    straggly tree
A stained slab blazoned with his strong and
    simple name
Rank grass and a mottled railing and an
    empty urn

The sturdy yeoman bones are mortared in the
    mountain
Rolled beneath the nettles with the stubborn
    bones of the Saxon
With the blunt and rasping bones of the
    scarred old Roman
With the brittle ringing bones of the arrogant
    Briton

Here he would canter his tubby pony through
    the bracken
To mark the cantilena in the wind's raw
    bluster
Or hark to the jog and jingle of the Welsh
    carter's horses
And place the man's rough whistle in a nest of
    strings

He would watch from the ledge in the rustle
    of the gorse
And catch the clack of the hawk as it furrowed
    down the breeze

And the hiss of the eagle stooping at its
    prey
And the easy lisp of the streams in the
    meadows below

Sometimes riding or driving across the dry
    and spiky country
Being Welsh and kin to the carter and the
    echoing bones in the hill
I sing a snatch of that striding eight-note
    melody
Diving down from the heights like the hawk
    flung from its perch

And parched with longing I see the vale of
    Malvern
And the scrawny tree above the forgotten
    contented grave
And hear again the dewy song of the
    blackbird
The tingle of the streams and the scrape of
    the wind in the bushes

I wander again in the heather on a morning
    bright with rain
The mountain rearing its square dark head in
    the push of the tune
The whole wet fragrant landscape caught in the
    shape of the fugue nobilmente
The sweep and surge of the hills and the mild
    soft thundery valley

All his music brings back the fond cracked
    voices of Britain
Compounded like bones in the old Silurian
    mountain

But this can tap and drum on the dusty
    heart
Till the sting of tears and the cool green
    memories come

A LETTER FROM THE CAFÉ DU MONDE

The tables on the sidewalk at the Café du Monde
    are steeped in the sunlight as I sit and dip
    my roll in my morning coffee

The coffee from the clattering French Market whose
    beans are cut by steel and blended with a
    pungent mixture of chicory

The special brand of coffee which will render the
    wearisome journey you asked about well worth
    the time and effort

The coffee the aproned waiters chatting in their
    cajun French serve with a plate of the famous
    fattening fragrant beignets of the Café du Monde

The fine strong coffee whose sinewy steam rivals the
    smoke of the ships across the bay and the thudding
    locomotives of the Southern Pacific

The steam as warm and fragile in my coffee cup as
    the wreath of tender thoughts it carries towards
    you

The steam that will lend an incense and urgency
    to the coffee-impregnated pages I will scribble
    and stuff in the airmail envelope

The letter you will slit with a lazy nail as you sip
    your café au lait in the sunlight of a city
    four thousand miles away

Adieu madras adieu foulards
Adieu rob'soie et colliers-choux

Doudou à moi il est parti
Hélas hélas c'est pour toujours

The sunlight is not the faded sunlight of our lost
    fond summers or the sun that will stroke you
    as you read my scrawl

The brazen American sunlight that slaps the flanks
    of the strapping bronze charger barrelling
    through Jackson Square

The electric southern sunlight that tickles the tip
    of the sword of the flourishing democratic
    general jammed in the saddle

The sunlight that peppers the Caesar salad of the
    magnolias and poinsettias and azaleas around
    the exuberant plinth

The aching sunlight that spices the wisteria trees and
    camellia trees rushing at the vibrating sky as no
    flowers ever sprouted in our wistful Europe

The heartless sunlight stinging my hand as it sprawls
    across the paper as it no no no no no not the
    soothing sunlight of Bougival and Neuilly

The sunlight that brushed the elegant soft grey nap
    of the waters of our distant darker decorous
    northern river

The sunlight that smoothed the summer afternoons in
    the mild sweet temperate days in the shadow of
    the willows

Adieu madras adieu foulards
Adieu rob'soie et colliers-choux
Doudou à moi il est parti
Hélas hélas c'est pour toujours

New Orleans is a handsome French city but not the
city in France where we lounged in the sunlight
and drank our morning coffee

New Orleans is a city where French is spoken but
not the light crisp laughing French you spoke
in the tender sun

New Orleans and Paris are only the width and price
of an airmail stamp apart but also the depth
of the heart and the breadth of the ocean

New Orleans is the place where I loiter in the
silly sunlight and drink my coffee and think
of the little tune we sang by the Seine

Adieu madras adieu foulards
Adieu rob'soie et colliers-choux
Doudou à moi il est parti
Hélas hélas c'est pour toujours

DEATH OF A RACING DRIVER

White the flashing helmet and the silk scarf sucked
in the mouth
Yellow the glimpse of soft leather gloves and the top
of the roll-neck sweater
Blue the blur of the denims and the flicker of tinted
lenses
Green the sleek smooth paint of the eloquent
machine
Black the tracks of the rubber scraping across the
road

Scarlet scarlet the flash of fire of the fuselage
striking the tree

Straight the sweep of the tarmac whirring past
the pits
Dipping the run downhill at the sharp right turn by
the lake
Curving the uphill pull with the throttle jammed
wide open
Serpentine and slow the gap through the
chicane
Sloping the treacherous camber at the corner under
the bridge

Crooked crooked the bend where the black
shreds point to the wreckage

Ripping the hungry engines waiting the fall of the
flag
Screaming the rising pitch on the blank mile past
the grandstand
Wailing of gears and tyres when the rear wheels
break away

29

Coughing and sobbing of failures like cougars with
broken backs
Howling the raging hunters charging along the
back-straight

Silence silence under the sodden boughs with the
ambulance-men in their oilskins

Wet and slick the surface below the hissing
spokes
Slippery the shuddering wheel beneath the dampened
fingers
Streaming the muddy windshield with oily beads
of spray
Sopping the visor and harness and supple calfskin
boots
Spongy the ruptured verge where the black streaks
run off the road

Dripping dripping the pine-trees above the
fuming embers

VERACRUZ

With rudder snapped and splintered oar
The boat lies empty on the shore
   Winds beyond the reef may roar
The boat will never venture more

   Silver fish may dart in droves
Gulls may slant their wings above
   The boat will never longer rove
Her sails are split and sides are stove

   Leave the wreckage where it lies
Beneath the salt and sullen sky
   Let the lazy sands drift high
Athwart her timbers flaked and dry

   She tore the skin from scores of hands
And strove to feed a starving land
   Now she rots upon the strand
Her rivets bleeding on the sand

   Her peeling flanks resist the lures
Of tides which vex the ocean floor
   Heedless on the vacant shore
The boat will never venture more

ACAPULCO

The rays of the calm disk enfold the vacant firmament
  Nothing disturbs the peaceful valleys of the ocean
The innocent beaches are neither scraped nor trodden
  The rocks are ripe and riddled with tender lucid pools
The sands are bright and unsoiled and empty
  The sea is guiltless
The clean edges of the beams of the sun-disk cast their
                    geometric rule

A bundle of feathers drops softly through the atmosphere
  A dolphin snorts and flops and shakes the seadew from
                    his back
A brilliant snake furrows a path across the lip of the
                    water
  A lizard fidgets in a comfortable crack in the rock
A starfish is imprinted like a jewel on the sand
  Whales squeak and wallow in a trough in the wave
The sky is filled with the whistle and flip of wings

A dashing young man who likes to drive fast has
                    harnessed the orb of the sun
  A ponderous old gentleman splashes about in the deep
A smiling self-regarding slightly cross-eyed girl is
                    stepping ashore
  Coiling on a warm smooth rock to dry her tunic and curl
                    her tousled hair around a lazy finger
The bleat of a conch floats in from far out across the
                    sprightly wave
  Drowning the hoofbeats of the ivory horses treading
                    above in the clouds

The silver wedge of a jet buzzes towards its ceiling
  A white yacht rides at anchor on the rim of the ocean
Surfers rocket landward through the booming scud

32

Cheered by the watchers lolling on the rocks
The beach is strewn with crumpled cartons and Coca-Cola
                bottles
Laughter ripples along the water from the swimmers
                plopping off the rafts
The sky is faintly hazy but gives almost no hint of rain

Violently a black tempest crashes from the heavens
    The seas are curdled with a sudden abominable storm
Squeals and panic on the beaches
    Cursing and sliding on the rocks
Desperate splashing through the breakers
    The white yacht slips its cable and vanishes in the
                bitter spray
A sulphurous tumult is blotting out the universe

Acid rains have scoured the pleasant heaven
    Sodden and scalded birds lie scattered on the sea
The serpent on the strand is blistered and raw
    The lizard on the rock is shrivelled
The dolphin rolls belly upward in the sullen ocean
    The sky is scissored and void of gulls

The young man unbridles the ivory horses and traipses
                home
    The jolly old gentleman gives up his games in the deep
The girl strolls down the beach to test the water with
                a reluctant pink toe
    Then dawdles back to the rock to collect her comb and
                her tunic
Returns to the water and wades out under the waves
    Leaving the landscape empty beneath an empty sky

The beams of the sun shed their straight light
    The sea is guiltless
The sands unstained

The rocks cupped with lukewarm pools
The beach unscratched by shell or print
The plain of the sea peaceful and untilled
The rays of the disk embrace a vacant firmament

AURORA

I

You above all I shall find it easy to remember
    Because I lost you between the swaying poppies
        and the tender volutes
And never recovered you though I sought you
        resolutely
    In the cave festooned with the soft weeping
        stalactites
And the cavern beyond it enclosing the secret
        rockpool

Somewhere between the sigh of the forest and the
        mutter of the waterfall
    In the corinthian darkness with the sweet dew
        dropping
And the giant cup spilling over into the swollen
        lake
    You fled away from me through a quivering tunnel
        of tendrils
Down chalky corridors carved through ghostly cliffs

Sometimes I utter a sleepy cry in the hooded
        darkness
    Straying down valleys and combing the velvety
        harvests
Sometimes I hunt you with fierce unyielding
        abandon
    Crushing the sappy grasses and bruising the
        innocent reeds
Crashing like a stark tusked animal through the
        scented springing bracken

Once we entered that hidden country hand in
        hand

Treading the quaking mosses with gay resilient
          steps
But now we slip over the border by separate
          paths
   And never encounter each other in all that
          marshy fastness
Divided by the matted banks of the buried river

What else can I do but stumble on and seek
               you
     Under the tumid buds on the furry feathered
          branches
Slithering over boulders damp with spray
   Climbing the shrouded hillside above the
          fecund ocean
Under the moist radiance of a melting moon

II

When slowly under me I see your blue
Eyes shut and lose you while possessing you

In that colossal landscape into which you suddenly
Leap and escape from being close to me

Entering that private country where I never know
          your real
Name or real face or body or how you feel

Or whose name it is you call out under the wide
          caress
Or the deep cry you utter when you sob and bless

O in that secret place where do you wander
Madam and haunt and taunt me keeping us asunder

Do you walk in scarlet there or run in white
Or simply lie asleep as naked as the night

Do you drink blood or water or champagne
Skip in the sun or loiter in the rain

Do you stand still or clap your hands and sing
Or lead a lion on a slender string

Madam madam O tell me what your blue
Eyes can see in that kingdom that belongs to you

While here I lean above you waiting to welcome
You from that far bright and blissful country home

III

If I could say something to you directly
Something perfect and simple and straight out
            of the heart
Something plain and without extravagance
Something without arrangement or artifice of
            any sort

If I could put the palm of my hand on the
            palm of your hand
Press the tips of my fingers against your
            fingertips
Lying with my cheek and hip and shoulder
            against your flank
Loose in the long and lazy nuzzle of your lips

If I could find a few clear and sufficient phrases
Proper words in proper order with nothing
            superfluous
A brief inevitable sentence to please and pierce
            you

A few right syllables profounder than prose or
                verse

It would make no difference to how you lean
                towards me
Returning my caress with joy and grace
Moving and opening your limbs with nothing except
                a sigh
Turning towards me with love and silence in your
                face

Yet I would like for once just once and only once
To be done with the dance of words that does no
                good
And give myself like you in your woman's wisdom
To the whirl and wildness of the wordless dance
                in the blood

TRANS-TEXAS

And then the machine collected its manifold forces and
Hurled itself at the sky and in sixty seconds the

City was children's bricks and the traffic was only
Dinkitoys and the earth receded a million

Years for every thousand feet until the landscape was a
Painting by Gris or Villon and a painting by

Gris or Villon was the landscape and the face was
Revealed of an earth which our fathers never

Imagined and which we never suspected as we drove to the
Airport that morning in our enamelled

Machines and certainly never expected to view in its
Seamed and muddy decrepitude with the

Volcanic wrinkles of canyons and mountains and lakes dried
Up long ago when the globe was wild and

Wet and young and then all that too was hid—
Den as the plane lifted to thirty thousand

Feet and the pattern of hills and valleys was
Repeated in white on the clouds down below and a

Miniature blue-and-red pinwheel of a sun was
Fixed on a cloud like a lapel-button and our

Little impudent urchin shadow emerged again and we sud-
Denly found ourselves where the angels used to sing and

Swing in their ancient dominion and if we were
Good we would fly there ourselves when we rose from our

39

Tombs but this morning their kingdom though
Vast and roomy enough for all of us was

Empty now and if we wanted to reach them we
Would have to fly to the far end of the universe and take

Care of falling like shining Satan thirty thousand
Feet like a streaming white candle and

TULAROSA

If we could read

If we could read the runes
Scraped on the patient sands and pliant dunes

Or climb a mountain's shoulder
And read the jottings on a jutting boulder

Or read the hieroglyphs
Carved in the hills and chiselled on the cliffs

Or trace the cuneiform
The lightning-flash embosses on the storm

Or understand the words
In those lost languages of winds and birds

Or know the verbal root
Locked in the ponderosa's knotted foot

Or recognize the mark
Stamped like an ideogram upon its bark

Or learn the shadowed message
Tossed like a teasing inkblot from its branches

Or some way could decipher
The secret perfume of the juniper

Or read as in a cup
The riddled leaves it scatters from its top

If we could read

If we could read the runes

NEW YEAR'S DAY
1969

There is a corona around the about-to-be-insulted moon
   The moon on which men will be dying soon
The moon will be blue in June

Walking at Ventura along the insulted sand
   I knew the era of the insulted ocean was over and the
                          era of the insulted land
And the era of the insulted empyrean was at hand

A world was shedding its divinity
   The last bright speck and shred of its virginity
And was about to sacrifice infinity

No more no more the pure and crystal music of the spheres
   Nothing but crapulous wisecracks from the farthest stars
Transistors crackling and cackling on Venus and Mars

It will be the greatest date they say since Columbus or
                      Christ
   The birth of welfare and the death of the priest
The start of the public world and the end of the private
                    world at least

Must it be therefore always for a poet to lament
   While mankind enters its new element
And ask if this is what Copernicus and Newton really meant

Diana is dropping a final maiden tear
   Her broken bow is slipping through the atmosphere
It drifts and disappears

We have poked and fingered those alabaster bubs
   Man is the creature who tampers and disturbs
Ravishes and robs

We have pitched our infected darts into the innocent fortress
　We have photographed the pockmarks of the huntress
Changed her from a goddess to a waitress

I watch beyond the purple wave
　The simple holy circle pale and grave
Wilt and regret like me the loneliness we cannot have

Although the sanctuary is vacant now and soiled and dim
　I raise my head and lift towards it one last time
The tribute of an evening hymn cast in a dying rhyme

Date Due